Poems from
San Francisco

Poems from San Francisco

COLE FELDMAN

CONTENTS

~

"Suppose a human being has thus put his ear, as it were, to the heart chamber of the world will and felt the roaring desire for existence pouring from there into all the veins of the world, as a thundering current or as the gentlest brook, dissolving into a mist—how could he fail to break suddenly? How could he endure to perceive the echo of innumerable shouts of pleasure and woe in the "wide space of the world night," enclosed in the wretched glass capsule of the human individual, without inexorably fleeing toward his primordial home, as he hears this shepherd's dance of metaphysics? But if such a work could nevertheless be perceived as a whole, without denial of individual existence; if such a creation could be created without smashing its creator—whence do we take the solution of such a contradiction?"

— Friedrich Nietzsche, *The Birth of Tragedy*

~1~
GOING NOWHERE FAST

FOUR OF US FEELING GOOD

Passing through a tunnel
under the low yellow lights
crossing the bridge smoking
in the car speakers drumming
early in the afternoon four
of us talking and feeling good
going straight on the road
trying not to think about
where we're going.

DRIVING FAST

Waxed wheels on
lighted asphalt just
waiting to rip a tread
in the dashed lines,

off to a point
in the dark pinched
distance, where other
racers wait saying,

Come on, catch up.

Grip the steering wheel,
but not too tight;
you can't let them see
that you're trying.

Lean back and careen
into the dark night.

SITTING ON THE OVERPASS

How much goes
in between cars

as we sit on
the overpass

dangling our legs
over the highway

counting
the seconds

sometimes much
sometimes little

until the traffic jam
during rush hour

when our work
is done too

and we get up
off the overpass

to walk on
the sidewalk home.

ALONE ON THE MAIN ROAD

Some several weeks pass when all I'm doing is ignoring, like a horse with blinders just trying to get along, walking straight down the main road and past forks, trails in the snow that lead nowhere.

I put my head down and pull my collar up around my neck, walking alone against the wind. Even though some of the false paths seem to lead somewhere sunny and warm,

I've got to keep on the main road and move forward not sideways, until I get to the real turn where the main road itself bends in a direction, and then I'll know for sure that's the way.

But the longer I trek, the more promising each of these premature paths appear. Sometimes I even try to trick myself into not seeing that the main road continues, and believing this false bend is really the one.

Though I know, if I ever turned off and got lost going the wrong way, I'd wonder about the main road and think of where I might've gotten if I'd carried on. So I pull up my collar and press on against the wind.

FLY BY NIGHT

Flying in the deep dark night
past fears of failure and falling,
none of which much matter

now that the rain beats into
the windows, and the horizon
is speckled with black clouds.

We speed on, wheels off the rails,
like a bullet train out of a pistol tunnel
gunning fast for an inevitable leap

straight out of reality, into a world
where the climbing higher, takes on
meaning, beyond just the physical.

HEARING THE HEIGHTS

No matter how many times
the sun rose
consistently in the morning
and the river flowed
in the same direction,

the order in the universe
still wasn't enough
to sustain a sense of meaning
that we could
wrap our heads around

in order to get on living
in the same direction
of hope for a future
that wouldn't let us down

like all the times
when we thought
we had something,

but it turned out
to be proven wrong,
or just simply forgotten

so that we've ended up now
as a group of individuals
locked in our own generation
stepped down from giant shoulders

and trying to hear for ourselves
what the heights have to say.

PLANE CRASH

Sometimes
I sleep soundly
on a plane ride,
when I'm all too
comfortable to die.

Otherwise
I worry about
a crash, of course,
as all people do.

I can't sleep;
I can't read;
I just sit there,

waiting for time
to move slower
than usual, jumping
at any turbulence

watching nervously
out the windows
as the wings
flex in the wind.

THE RIGHT WAY

All around me
are traps and snares;

only one way
is the right one
and it's not straight,

so always, I must
keep my eyes wide open

—or I'll move, when
I'm supposed to stay
or turn left, when
it's the other way

and just stopping
or turning around
aren't options,

until that's what
the right way tells me.

HIKING

Looking out
at the open ocean,

I'm not sure
which side
is the sky,

where the line
between water
and air, watching
feet touch trail

as our progress
goes unnoticed,

save focus
on the presents
that were passing,

even though
the passage itself
made no difference
to the hike ahead,

carrying us along
inside a sublime
physical world.

COLORADO LEAVES

A big tree, across the street;
an oak, I don't know.

It's October in Denver
and the leaves are shades
of green, orange, and yellow.

One branch has green leaves
that are all young—a school
of youths without elders.

Another has mostly orange
—middle-aged citizens,
thinking back to being green
in their spring months.

And the yellow leaves
—nearing the end of their lives,
looking to the ground below
and preparing for their Fall.

IN BETWEEN SEASONS

On a sunny afternoon in March, sitting on a bench in South Park, between second and third street in San Francisco, this occurs to me.

That it is never in the middle of a season that I can discern its identity. In the middle of a season it seems to be just the way things are.

But in between, when two seasons are still deciding whose turn it is to play, playing tug of war, winter and spring,

such that the days before this were all rainy, dark, and dreary, and the weatherman said this morning that the days after today will go back to the same.

In this back and forth, it is clear to see what the seasons are like. As the dark closes in and keeps pointed all that the light opens up and lets out.

On a sunny day like today, I am open. I can see more. In the open hot sun, the brightness shows to me finer features that are hidden in the dark,

as parts of general black masses or concealed in ambiguous shadows, like at night with your eyes closed before bed, as you think inward into yourself.

Hibernating in the winter, adding to and bolstering your ego, to warm up in the spring, and let it all go in the summer.

HOMECOMING

Standing on the back porch
hearing the *chk-chk* of sprinklers,
smelling the fresh-cut grass,
and feeling the summer air.

Seeing the distant horizon
over plains, past the pond;

remembering what it was like
to grow up here—barefoot,

with the front door unlocked;
and how much has changed.

I think of when my parents
left their homes, when they
were my age, and if they ever

returned from their travels
and stood on the back porch
of my grandparents' house,

trying to reconcile, the rest
of the world, with what they
grew up, thinking was everything.

LEAVING

I pack my bags and
find among my things
what my life has become
since the last time I left.

~2~
WORKING IN THE CITY

THE SOCIAL MAN

The social man, seen to be with people, makes me wonder why they love him. Why they hang on his arms and laugh at his jokes. Whether it is superficial or genuine—either is good enough reason apparently.

The lights get bright and conversation gets louder when he walks into the room; they either want to impress him subtly or to get his attention outright.

The social man is attractive, if only by virtue of seeing that others are attracted to him. If seen alone, it would ruin everything for the social man.

Any man alone, even a socialite, looks like a leper, without a partner to invoke his social qualities.

GROCERIES ON THURSDAY

In the city, there are unspoken rules about where people ought to be at certain times of the day

—for example, on a weekend night, the bars are full; and on weekday mornings, coffee shop lines are the longest; and on Saturday around noon, it's tough to get a table at the best brunch spots;

and after five on Friday, when everyone gets off work, you can count on bumper to bumper traffic on the highway out of the city; and at four in the morning, if you're not in bed, it's nerve-racking to pass by anyone else who's still awake on the sidewalk.

Last Thursday, I took a sick day from work, but was feeling good enough to get out of bed and go to the grocery store at 10:41 in the morning—I remember because, before I wrote this, I looked at my black digital Casio watch that cost $7.54 (or something like that, what with the taxes added I can't remember exactly).

The normal time to get groceries is after working hours, or on Sunday night when you've procrastinated all weekend but need to stock your fridge before the week, because you won't have time and will want something to eat when you get home from work each night.

So, on a Thursday morning at 10:41, it was odd to find people at the grocery store, other than myself. Knowing my own reason for being there, having called off sick from work, I wondered about the others—

whether they had jobs, and if not, where did they get their money from; and whether they had families, and if so, who made the money for the family?

There was a sense that they were out of place or off track, and I even started to feel guilty myself like we were all somehow breaking the rules.

But what a place built for so much with so little! All the shelves stocked and the produce section with mounds of fruit stacked and balanced perfectly.

I even avoided buying apples, even though they were on my list, because I was afraid of taking one from the top and all the rest would come crashing down—how embarrassing that would be!

See, I'm one of these normals, usually on the trodden track, so when I looked at all the open space and quiet there—and could push my shopping cart freely without having to say "excuse me," in a place designed for the mad rush of the after-work crowd, or for Sunday evening when chores are done according to the norms—it made me a little nervous.

SUCH STEEL

In a city full of people, steel stands straight up
to support an industrial flow of life

above on the streets and in the buildings, where
bodies come in contact all day;

some stay supple and human, while others
become like the steel and part of the foundation

—in one way, they have given in to the machine
and forfeited their humanity;

in another, they have made a great sacrifice for
those of us who choose to remain supple,

like the Dionysian man who would otherwise
dance and sing, overwhelming his bounds,

and paying no attention to what is required for
his survival, working up his appetite

until he would eventually lose all his humanity
and even eat his neighbor,

without the economic Apollonian steel, to
structure and point his passions.

HOMO CIVITAS

For those babies born
in the hospital downtown

taking their first steps
on paved cement

surrounded by street lights
and planes overhead

(even the plants
are placed there!)

everything designed
by landscape architects

and erected by men
in orange vests

jackhammering already
jackhammered roads

and cranes, almost as many
as buildings, in the skyline

—the city is home for
man that makes himself.

SAFE ON THE SIDEWALK

We walk on the sidewalk
and don't step out onto the street
to avoid getting hit by a car.

Everywhere, we walk on sidewalks
to safely get where we're going.

I wonder about the alternate routes
and the walks on the other side.

Sometimes I linger,
letting my feet touch the edge,
wondering what it would be like
to take the hit, just once.

RUNNING

Running from my apartment at 8th and Harrison to the gym on Market between 3rd and 4th over puddles from last night's January rain on the sidewalk waiting at the stoplight past a bakery on Folsom with good smells on Saturday morning and a sign that says "where good friends and beautiful girls meet" past the sandwich shop where I usually get a ginormous turkey sandwich for lunch on Saturdays but I'm still full from breakfast past a homeless man sitting with his back against the window of a storefront and his eyes looking down and across the street at the light to the right side just to keep moving even though up ahead I need to make a left turn and finally a straight away shot on the sidewalk with almost nobody in the way so I can really take off and stretch my legs looking up to pace for the light at the next stop and looking down trying not to step on the cracks just like the childhood game and all the way for a while because in San Francisco it's only about ten blocks that it takes to make a mile until I come up to the next light at 5th street now close enough to where I need to cross over and turn left and my luck is good for the light to go left to say "walk" with the little white man lit up instead of the red hand saying "stop" but I run instead of walking across Folsom and then up 5th towards Market dodging around shoppers stepping out of stores on their cell phones not paying attention until right on Market practically having to walk now all the people playing drums on buckets for coins selling stolen items walking hand in hand preaching traffic cop whistle blowing camera picture taking aching homeless always aching picking up speed for the last leg until I see my doorman waving smiling holding an open door.

CAPITALIST VALUES

I have some capitalist values,
like the inclination to break things
because I can replace them.

Or, when something doesn't work,
to move onto the next, rather
than trying to fix the first.

When something does work well
and isn't broken, I want more,

more and more, until I'm putting
anything and everything into the factory
just to have more of that one thing.

SUNDAY MORNING

Openness tells me, there
is still more to be gotten
from a week that's either
over or just beginning.

While weekend-waiters
wait wanting, awake
in their beds.

Wide stretches of road
when city cars are still
sleeping in their garages.

Stores without shoppers,
sidewalks with no walkers,
and views of a blue sky
clear of building tops.

~3~
SITTING IN THE APARTMENT

MY WHOLE APARTMENT

Sometimes it seems small; when I've gotten used to it and know every square inch—

when I've come home from work at the exact same time and cooked the same dinner

and lighted the same candle and meditated on the same cushion at the foot of my bed—

it seems to fold in on itself. I get claustrophobic and push on the walls to let in some air.

Other times, I have to stand taller to touch the ceiling; my bookcase seems to have another shelf

and the art pieces that I have hanging become like windows, opening my walls to other worlds.

When I look closely enough, it's really myself that starts to feel small,

like I could run for miles, and never get from my bed to the bathroom.

SHOWER FAUCET

The world is laid open
in brief moments of clarity.

An ordinary shower faucet
says to me, *How interesting?*

I look at its ordinariness
and respond silently, *Very.*

CEILING LIGHT

I turn on a dim light;
dim at first, then bright,
once my eyes have adjusted.

So I look up at the bright light
and say, "Who are you?"

And he says in reply,
"I am the same. It is you
who have changed."

I *hmph* and cross my arms;
why are lights always right?

BOILING WATER

Watching the water boil, I realize I am usually doing something else, like cutting an onion.

Now that I actually take the time to watch, as bubbles cover the pot's floor

and the first few crawl up the sides, I feel a little fear, like an explosion is imminent.

Silently and drawing me in, until the bubbles waiting on the floor begin to rise—slowly at first

and then all at once; the surface explodes with noise (and the awareness that it was silent before)

—which is what usually draws my attention away from cutting the onion

and so then I start to see what I've already seen so many times before.

Turned around, doing something else, how many other small explosions do I miss?

A HAT

A hat I haven't
worn for a while

hangs on the rack
begging to stay.

He opens his brim
and sings baritone,

"A hat like me
is an opportunity,

to cover upside down
or fill right side up:

a head of brains
or a bucket of rain;

a top for a party
or a pail of life
for a little garden."

I tell him, with
a somber tone,

"I can't keep you,
hat, you know this.

The girls didn't like
you, the last time we
went out together."

He doesn't get
angry, just sad,

and droops there
on the rack,

waiting for when
I can take him out,

but I might just
leave him; there

are enough sad
hats in the world.

LIGHT SWITCH

A light switch
in the dark
after sleeping
two light switches
actually
one on top
of the other
lighted barely
in the dark
not by themselves
of course
nor by the light
they control
in the bedroom
but from the light
in the bathroom
controlled
by another switch
that I now see
when I wash my hands
after sleeping
which drives me
to write
about a light switch
after some time
unproductive.

DISHWASHER MUSIC

I turn on the dishwasher before bed to work while I sleep. This makes me happy—something that is beautiful and also productive, like a domestic symphony

making music and cleaning at the same time. She talks to me like my mother—reassuring me after my nightmares with soothing sounds of a storm.

I sleep for a little while, listening to the splashing of water against dishes like rain on the roof, but then all of a sudden, I wake and wonder, *What is it like to be a dish in the washer?*

I've never done it, I realize. Never put myself through the terror to which I subject my utensils and wares. After thinking of this, I can't get any sleep.

I get out of bed in the dark and go over to sit on the floorboards in front of the dishwasher and wait anxiously for the load to run.

As soon as I get the green light, I open the door and pick up a bowl and ask, *How was it in there?*

The bowl says nothing. I ask again, *Hey, I'm worried about you and the rest of the set. Is everything alright in there?* Still, the bowl says nothing.

So I stack it gently in the cupboard and whisper, *I'm sorry,* making a silent promise to wash the poor bowls by hand from now on.

FRIDGE TALKING

Such silence
after the noise

of the refrigerator
working to freeze water

or whatever it is
that a fridge does
whirring in the night

making noise
that you don't realize
is noise

until the click
that turns it off

and then real silence
at 3:25 a.m.

no cars outside
oh, there went one
on California street

now silence again
as the low hum
of nothingness

makes me wonder
if silence has a sound

if hearing nothing
is like seeing nothing,

seeing black, hearing
with your eyes closed

oh, a plane,
I think—
something above
—gone now

and the hum again
no, her breathing
against my chest

always a noise
to fill the silence
if you really listen.

DRYER CLICKS

The dryer stops running and there sounds a *click*, which is the door unlocking—this is my cue to get up and fold the dry clothes.

I don't, however, or at least, not right away. Instead, I sit and enjoy the silence in the apartment, now that the load has run.

But then I hear another *click*, which is when I get confused; because it is always the same, after thirty-six minutes of *whrr, whrr, whrr, whrr*—

then the whirring stops, and the door unlocks, but just once. So that now, upon hearing the second *click*, I'm perplexed.

A dryer is a mechanical thing and can only click as it is made to—and just then, as I had this thought, there was a third *click*! So I listened closer

and heard not only the *click's* but also the subtle *rgg's* and *prrt's* that are the same as a runner saying *ahhh* after a race, or a lawyer saying *phew* after a case.

So I said, alright, alright, and got up off the couch to open its lid smiling smugly and then see its happy belly lit by a dim yellow light

displaying proudly for me a perfectly dry mound of clothes. "Thank you," I said. And just then, two *click's*, that sounded a lot like, "You're welcome."

WOODEN STOOL

I kicked some dust bunnies under the sofa, but my legs were getting tired, so I looked for a place to sit.

He seemed to be asking for it, but I wanted to make sure first, so I asked, "Can I sit here?"

He didn't say anything, until I prodded and he said, *wood*. "Yes, I know *wood*, but may I sit here?"

I asked. He didn't answer. So I prodded again and he said, *wood*. That was it, I guess.

So I invented up questions like, *What are trees made of?* To make the conversation go smoother.

SUCH A DOOR

Keep me up all night, alright, I get it, but you don't have to be such a door about letting people pass through just to get where they're going, when they might even give you a nice wave if you'd let 'em.

But you're so stuck on being closed all the time, and forcing people to reach out and pay tribute to your function, when you could just do what you're supposed to and pay it no mind and save your energy for staying open as long as you possibly can.

"What if I don't want to?" she asked, wriggling her handle and swaying on her hinges.

"Well don't then! See if I care. Plenty of open doors in this building." I threw up my hands in disgust and walked away, putting the wall between us.

What'd I think I was going to get out of talking to a door anyway?

KITCHEN WINDOW

Standing in the kitchen as my tea steeps, I look to my left through a window in the wall, which seems to be a picture, even though every part of it has a whole life of its own, that you'd know firsthand, if you were outside, up close.

The birds that are black dots in the distance are really birds, and they would *squawk* and fly up into the ceiling if they were in your living room. The leaves that are smudges, moving with the wind, you could smell their teeming green life, if you held them in your hand.

The people that walk on the sidewalk, that you could aim at if you were a sniper in a war, without ever knowing them—the very same people that you could have over on the couch to join you for tea and ask about where they come from and what they like doing and perhaps they would answer you and perhaps you and they would become friends.

In the window, however, it is all faraway and unreal; just colors that sometimes move (if you really think about it, when you have too much time on your hands, waiting for your tea to steep).

The movement is the only thing that tells you a story other than a talented painter has used the outsides of your windows as canvas. And if you spend any more time inside alone—as more time passes since the last bird you heard *squawk*, the last leaves you smelt, and the last people you met—then you might really start to believe it about the painter.

~4~
IN AND OUT OF LOVE

CELESTIAL LADDER

Our souls climb the celestial ladder
with time to finish what we started,
in the early budding flower season

when all loves are happy, just by virtue
of two humans, having come together.

Higher, here—things are more dire now,
and the stakes are raised on both sides.

Deeper into the more than divine sky,
before crashing earthward back into
a very physical, almost primal nature,

concerning ourselves with only
bodies that we can touch and see,

which is certainly a step back
from the sublime godly life
that our love had taken on.

CLIPPED WINGS

I carry a capturing device in my heart, that catches what my mind can't;

when words don't make sense, all that I have— other than a kiss and a touch

—is to try and say something, using words like clipped wings, whispering and waiting

to see if she watches, for the next vowel on my rounded lips. I could not tell her what I mean,

only that I do really mean it. Mumbling and trying not to touch, trying to start

softly and politely with my words, like wine before dinner. Charging up my fingertips

like batteries, with energy from the space in between our skin, waiting for her to feel the potential

and want for it like a magnet. I wait and wait, forever if I have to.

PRETTY GIRL

I lay out on my balcony,
perfectly fine and alone,
enjoying the sun, tanning,
minding my business.

On the balcony across,
a pretty girl steps out
to hang her laundry.

I shield my eyes and look
away, but it's too late.
Now I'm thinking of her;

I try, but fail, to think
of anything else.

I huff, get up, and go inside
to distract myself
with something else.

CUTE COFFEE GIRL

Cute coffee girl, drawing.
Everyone else, talking.
Me, working up the courage
to write her this poem.

FRECKLE STARS

I try to memorize
her freckles,
like a sky of stars

so that when
I'm not with her,

I can close my eyes
and place
the constellations

—two on the upper
inside of her left breast,

and a trio in the center
of her collarbone;

like they were placed
there, by design.

TWO AS ONE

When to stay
and when to go;

when to reap
and when to sew.

When to laugh
up a daffodil,

and when to cry
down an ocean sky.

For me it seems
that all is two—

save what is one,
save me and you.

A LOVE LETTER

I wanted to say I love you, but couldn't because I wasn't worthy of you. So I went away to improve myself. But am now realizing there is much more to improve before I am worthy of you. And it's going to take some time. And I can't stand to be near you in the meantime. Because it only makes me want you more. And I can't stand to hear about the other people you're with. And I know you need a lot. And I want to become all of that. But it's going to take some time. And even if on your doorstep years from now I'm still not enough, I'll have to live with that. And if you're with someone else, I'll have to live with that too. And if you didn't even want me in the first place, and even after all my work you still don't want me, well I suppose it might kill me—and if it doesn't, at least I'll have something to do until I get too old to love anymore. But right now, I can't say I love you and mean it, and that's the only way I can stand to be with you. Oh, and one last thing: thank you. Most of the time it hurts, but to love like this, I think is the closest thing to the meaning of life I've ever felt.

WRITING FOR HER

She makes me write
what the world can read,
so she can see
what they think of me.

Otherwise, I would
write only for myself,
and go off alone.

I wish she would
see it on her own,
what only I see.

But alas, here I am,
writing for them.

SAY IT

You say you do, but
I don't think you do,
really, want to say
what you're about to.

Some things said
can't be taken back;
even though the same
goes for silence,
so you're trapped.

GONE GIRL

Wave goodbye
all teary-eyed

in lieu of what
you promised.

Remember me
like you do.

Hold onto the hue
that we created

under the pretense
that you would
never leave.

Go on then,
I'm bitter already.

PLAYING WITH FIRE

Iced stuff over the fires that could have burnt anything but this. The contrast, miraculous. To see her fight, not to fall into this love. No, any one but this one.

To dissolve into someone else, to become like water that is shaped by the glass of another, and then to have that glass break—where then is the water to go?

So that choosing this, is like placing papier-mâché into a fire, and wondering after, why would we have built it, only to give it away? Just for a flash in the pan—or, for a fire that really burns.

Even when the fuel runs out. Choosing probable death, of what you previously called yourself, that has now become a half, and can no longer survive without the other.

LOVED AGAIN

I stepped low
and let the bass
in my feet
rumble.

I looked
into a like face
and loved
again.

I wanted to see
what was taken
from me
for the last time.

I've cared
for my queen
as I could.

WORLD FOR YOU

If I create
a world for you,
would you stay?

Or try and leave
on a cloudy day,

and steal away
with my favorite flower.

If you stayed,
would there be

enough room
for you
to dance around,

and enough space
to pay you attention;

would you miss
what you left behind?

Or climb the tallest tree
and smile at the sun,

happy with
the world you have.

LOVE

Do we change
until we become
someone that some-
body will love?

~5~
EVERYTHING IS ART

ALL THE ART I CANNOT SEE

It's on a good day,
the whole world
seems like art;

every word you say
sounds like poetry

and everything I see
looks like a painting.

I want to dance with couples
that are really just walking

and sing with strangers
that are really just talking.

I want to capture it all
in a jar, and seal the lid,

in order to somehow
save it for a rainy day

when I would otherwise
constantly say,
what else is there?

And miss all of it,
right in front of my face.

CARDBOARD BOX

On a good day,
I have no ability
to edit my work
because it all seems
great to me;

everything seems great,
even that cardboard
box over there—

I wonder if I could
break it down flat
and put it in a frame
to hang on the wall.

SATURDAYS

Saturdays are for art;
you don't have to maintain
yourself, this is the day

to let yourself go, and see
what you discover; you can
worry about everything else
during the work week;

on Saturday, just be happy
and marvel at everything,
no matter what it is.

WORLD EATER

An artist
is a world eater:

tasting and mulling
over old worlds,

chewing them up
with her canvas teeth,

mashing bits together
with her sculpting tongue,

puckering her painted lips,
and spitting out new worlds.

INEFFABLE ART

I see art in everything, that could just as easily be anything else, but it is what it is.

All that you have is here and now, no matter whatever is, elsewhere or elsewhen.

All I've ever written is the same thing, said different ways. Everything is art;

any argument I've heard otherwise, comes from our primitive need to classify and sort and make sense.

Everything is very interesting just as it is, and any creation of any kind is a contribution to what is—

which is art, all of it. It doesn't matter why, just that it is, so interesting—this, I try to describe,

while avoiding the temptation to overexplain, just because of my own need to understand.

AMORAL ART

I do not look
to say, *That is there.*
Only to say, *I see.*

I do not listen
to say, *That is true.*
Only to say, *I hear.*

I do not touch
to say, *That is right.*
Only to say, *I feel.*

All my art
says nothing
other than, *I am.*

NON-PROFIT ART

I don't mean to manipulate your attention by editing my experience—that seems to be more like mass-production than art. I have to keep it the way it appears to me, you see, looking through the only lens I'm given, running in whatever direction, regardless of its collisions with the world we know;

otherwise it ceases to be mine, even before it becomes yours, and then might as well be anything else—like a marketer careful to create only what will be consumed, with profit as muse; or a politician placing propaganda in your morning news.

No, there is only hope that you would wander after it all alone, unguided, and stumble upon what you might not have otherwise, and feel at first the jolt of surprise, and then a joy at having found, completely by accident, something of which you are rather fond.

But we must trade the possibility of never stumbling upon it in the first place, for the guarantee that, if you do happen to stumble upon something, it will not have been placed there in your track.

ABSTRACT ART

Lying in bed in the dark at night so I can "see" with my eyes closed

—my toes against each other, my legs against the bedsheets, and my hip bones against my skin.

I can only come up with a rough sketch that doesn't match the exact picture I've seen before

—from my memories of looking in the mirror at what is supposedly the real image of myself.

There is a certain emotion, still, that goes with even the roughest sketch.

Something that just barely looks like a face, but is really only the curve of one side of the jaw,

a shadow between the eye and the eyebrow, or a line where the forehead meets hair

—individually, these marks and shapes are nothing; together, however,

they represent all the faces that we've loved, hated, longed for, and feared.

~6~
WRITING ABOUT WRITING

PICKING POEMS

I go out to get a poem:
meet people, shake hands,
look around, and dance.

I look at things and
tilt my head to the side.

I lean off the edge
and listen for new words.

I let myself dabble in love
if only to get a poem of pain.

I hold a leaf and let it scratch
a sentence on my palm.

I get home and go to sleep,
too drunk to think of poetry,

then wake up with
a mind full of it,
at four in the morning.

There are no poems
I won't consider.

There are many things
I haven't seen.

I'VE GOT ONE

I would say that this has meaning but am timid, because of what I've called out before that didn't end up meaning much of anything—so I let it pass.

I would move on and forget, but once I try to turn to something else, I find it persisting and tugging like a child on my pant leg, crying and cooing or otherwise saying, "Look at me, I matter."

Still, I shake it out of my head to make space for what might come with real meaning—something that people will read and say, "Ah, yes, yes indeed, *that* means something."

But on the third time, as I try to push it away and move on to what might matter, I find that it has put down roots and grown—into something I didn't expect from its start as just a passing thought.

Now with all its weight and getting me excited, shouting in my face, "You fool, how could you not have seen before?"

So I scramble for my pen and paper like a fisherman with one on the line, cursing and murmuring to myself, "I've got one, I've got one."

POEMS NOT HEARD

One workday during lunchtime, I was walking down New Montgomery, and passed briefly in front of an alley. I saw a homeless man, standing with his shopping cart, and heard him say,

> *The first part*
> *is you have to go*
> *somewhere that knows.*

That's all he said, to nobody, as people passed by on the street; nobody was listening. His glossy eyes showed that he, also, was seemingly unaware of what he had just said. It took me a second to realize—

it is not uncommon for people on the streets in San Francisco to be talking to themselves

—but as I repeated it in my head, I found it to be quite good, and stopped, hoping that he would go on, but that was all he said, only once. So I repeated it out loud to myself:

> *The first part*
> *is you have to go*
> *somewhere that knows.*

I wondered if this was his only poem, or if there were others. I wondered if the most prolific poet in history could be a homeless man who nobody had ever heard of (or cared to listen to).

A WRITER

Even before, I told myself
I was—I still was, even then,
I think—and even when,
I wish I wasn't, I am then too.

Less so when I'm happy,
because it's hard to do any-
thing else when you're happy,
other than to be that way
—let alone to write.

Writers are not happy,
I find; unless they are,
then they really are.

SATISFIED

Funny, that
even satisfaction
becomes dissatisfying.

When I am happy
I think to myself,

*I could live on like this
and never write again.*

But then I wake
on a Sunday morning

with blank pages
and not even memories
of the last couple days.

I am dissatisfied
and so completes the circle;

I pick up my pen
and begin to write again.

ORDINARY POEMS

I wrote a hundred poems
to have meaning in every one,

but in the end, said to myself,
there's just not that much
meaning in the world.

So I learned to write
about ordinary things
and wouldn't you know,

I found all the meaning
underneath a flower pot
in the tool shed.

WRITING TO FORGET

My writing allows me
to deposit my memories
somewhere outside of myself.

I can forget them
and not feel guilty about
losing them forever.

I put them down on paper
and send them wherever
they need to go,

which is sometimes
the waste basket,
but even then,

I don't have to
carry them with me,
weighing me down.

WRITING THE WHALE

On a Saturday morning that you've taken off on your own to get out of the city and sit by the ocean to relax, you get this feeling that you've arrived.

Sitting on the rocks that border the beach near the wharf, you think to yourself, "I'd like to write," but you're not quite there yet.

If you wait, you'll see the crabs, convinced that you're not a bird, crawl out from their crevices, to eat the algae on the rocks,

so many of them that the rocks themselves seem to be moving, and you think to write then but ask yourself, "Wait, what if there's more?"

So you sit there silently instead, waiting, until you taste the salt in the air and want to write then, but wait, take off your shoes

to feel the sand in between your toes, and want to write then, but wait, fly up to grab one of the seagulls and let it *squawk* in your ear—

and keep waiting and floating and balancing like you're playing a memory game where one more thing is added, and another, and another,

until you can't bear it anymore and think you might just explode, but wait—

until you've really got the whole thing, and finally the whole whale comes up from the deep

and shatters the surface with a great big splash. Then you can really see what you've got.

Otherwise you only end up describing one point on the surface, like one scale from one fish out of the whole wide ocean.

If you come back into town with only one scale, no matter how real the great big whale was to you in the moment,

the townspeople will think up a fish totally different than the one you saw, and end up down a rabbit hole, guessing wrong.

There's nothing wrong with guessing wrong, but then they might as well have guessed anything at all, let alone what you went out to the wharf to see.

AUTO-POETRY

Sometimes I check my notepad,
in hopes that some poetry
has written itself for once.

~7~

CHRONOPHOBIA

NARROW DAYS

Tell me what
does become of
the narrow days

that pinch up all
the time between
morning and night

so that in the middle
there's a rushed river

that cuts deep and
doesn't leave room

for morning coffee
or nighttime tea,

but is instead
sandwiched for lunch
so tight in the middle

that when you go to bite
all you get is the thin air
rushing out of your lungs

on the last narrow day
that you didn't know
would be your last.

EARLY

In the early morning
when some of the night
is left over,

and the day hasn't quite
reached over the horizon,

an in-between world
where everything is still

takes hold
of the same terrain

where waking life
normally holds sway,

and you can't quite tell
if it's a human planet
because nobody's around.

NIGHT

Nights, like everything else, have their own slow beginnings. Nothing can start fast right away. It's got to first figure itself out, as a thing apart from other things.

For the night, this is clear, as the darkness sets itself apart from the light. It is most itself in the middle, darkest and alone. And then time will start to change it.

The changes happen faster and faster, until the original thing explodes into the next morning, and the night isn't itself anymore.

A myriad of other things, born from the explosion, seek their own slow beginnings, in the light of the new day, set apart from the dark.

NIGHT #2

What goes in these nights fighting
Age, the malaise of youths eldered
And all seeing the light of day
Consumed by nothing dark night

Fight these deep nights dark going
Elding youths no malaise, not yet
Not while hope of the day still lingers
Still beyond night's appetite for nothing

Beyond gnashing dark teeth like shadows
Inching, elding into the day's light at dawn
Nights that fight the dread dark coming
Fight while youthful hope still lingers

Fight the night bring light here brighter
Hope the hope that brings near wishers
Dream a dream beyond night's nothing
Young dear sweet bedmate keep beauty

In these nights whence light once rushed
Hoped in hearts as youths tend to
Kept in sight of the day's touch

Hold me here dear sweet young beauty
Tell me what goes in these nights fighting

GOD OF TIME

The God of time
talks in a rhythm,

matching the ticks
of his clock hands.

You shouldn't stop
when you need to go.

You shouldn't rest
when you need to wake.

Keep up, not too fast,
like this, *Tick … tick …*

TORN LIKE A SUNSET

Tell me things
about when they
weren't like this;

when you had to
dress a dandelion
just to hold down

the fort for a night's
forgotten cabin.

I miss those nights,
even the ones
that have yet to dusk,

that might resemble
nights gone past,
in which case
I can't wait.

Torn like a sunset,
nights are like dying,

which means they
are also like living.

I always
want it to start
but I never
want it to end.

PRESENT

The subtle present—
this we trade too readily
for a future that can't
possibly match our hopes:

a future that is really
just a present yet to pass.

PRESENT #2

Pushing back the past
and the future forward,

deep between narrow
canyon walls, the present
stretches out its arms—

like a young newcomer
pinched into oblivion
by colossal incumbents.

LIVING IN THE PAST

I wouldn't have wanted to think of it, had I any hope of experiencing it again, in the real world. Without such hope, all I had was the memory.

I know to avoid living in the past; in this case, however, even a hazy and abstract semblance was better than any present reality.

Lying in bed at night, I played it over like a movie on the backs my eyelids, until my memory was not even of the actual occurrence,

but more so a picture of a picture, like looking into one mirror with another behind you, on and on, smaller and farther away and more distorted.

Still, for what seemed like the longest while, there was nothing out in the city that seemed like it could be any better.

Only recently have some realities presented themselves as superior, so that I can finally get out of bed in the morning, and do something other than just lie there and try to remember.

SPENDING TIME

Now that it's over, even though I've been after it this whole time; apparently, I carried nothing along. So that I have nothing to show for my time, nothing to hold onto that I can touch and feel and say, "*This* is what I got for it." Only now that it's over do I feel this way. I can still remember moments while it was still going on, when I would have said "this is it" or "I feel good" or "oh wow." It is only in hindsight now that I wonder what was gotten, even though all along I would have told you that I was getting it, and even held you by the shoulders and exclaimed to you, "*This* is it!"

Perhaps it is a function of my bad memory that I now feel empty-handed. Or perhaps it is the nature of time to lock anything good in the present whence it passed, so that this present which now finds me writing—which was only a future from the perspective of the past present to which I am referring—is a whole thing in and of itself, which cannot contain any of the goodness from before. Like a banker with a vault, I keep putting funds into the vault, in an attempt to save, only to find that they disappear right away.

Time is not like money after all. It doesn't save. You have to spend it when you've got it. Spend it deeply and rightly and well. Don't expect to remember why you spent it or what you got for it, because at any time after, when you are thinking like this, and trying to remember what you spent your time doing, in that very moment you will have more time to spend, and you'll be better off just spending that time, rather than trying to remember how you spent your time before.

THINKING OF WHAT WILL BE

Experiencing what is, thinking of what will be, wondering how what is will affect what will be, letting your thoughts about what will be define your experience of what is, letting your feelings about what you are experiencing be good only in the case that they are good for what will be,

only allowing yourself to be a certain way, which is to say only allowing what there is to be a certain way, and making these requirements for yourself based on what you want yourself to be at some point in the future, which is to say making requirements for what will be in the future, trying to control the future.

All the time doing this in the present, to manipulate what will be in the future, instead of just allowing the present to be itself, and thus looking deeper into the experience of the present with your full self that also exists in the present.

Letting water run together with water, instead of always focusing the attention of your present self on thoughts of the future, letting water try but fail to run together with oil.

Future thoughts are merely experiences of a reality that has yet to pass, and thus are less clear and less real than the thoughts of a present reality that exists right in front of your nose, overwhelming your appetite for attention, over and over again, if you really look deep enough, and never run out of things to see.

OPEN YOUR EYES

When the past is
gone, it's gone.

When the ships have
sailed, they've sailed.

Whether it was or wasn't,
doesn't matter now.

When the meadowlark
moans, you must crane
your neck, and look up
into the tree, and see.

Your mind and memory
have failed you with facades
you'll never fully realize.

Lean in after the sight
and let it swallow you whole,

until you can no longer
tell the difference between
yourself and what you see.

When the past is gone,
it's gone. Let it go.

Open your eyes and see
what you have left.

OLD MAN

Aging, old man, looking back,
remembering, pulling forward;
what for, old man, what for?

Things are different now;
you are different now.

What you wish for isn't here,
can't be; it's back there, always.

With the same powers
that you look backwards,
look here—this is it.

What you long for, it is here.

Just as you were you
meeting what was; again,
you are you, here and now,
meeting what is.

TIME FILLED WITH SPACE

We tried to break each moment,
swinging space like a hammer
to smash apart anvil time.

Just as we were about
to have each moment full,
the next moment would begin
and all the air would let out

escaping into the previous
moment, that we had almost
already forgotten.

So we set out like Sisyphus,
filling up the next moment,
the next, and the next …

TIME MARCHES ON

Suppose you thought
the clock really cared,

ticking along like
a march of time soldiers
that the coldest winter
snow couldn't stop.

Even if Atlas himself
held back the clock hands
with all his strength,

it would take much more,
even more than the shoulders
that hoist the world,

to stop everything
from changing.

AFTER THIS

I like to find
I've opened time
and made it wide

so its passing
doesn't matter
anymore.

I like to hear
the clamor clear
and really start
to listen.

I like to hope
beyond hope
that after this
there is a this
still to be.

But then again
I start to sin
and stumble.

Which is when
I like to find
I've opened time
and made it wide

so its passing
doesn't matter
anymore.

~8~
META

MORENESS

Sometimes
I think to myself,
what if this is it?

Then I'm hit
with such a gust
of moreness,

that at first, I try
to catch my breath,

and then feel foolish
for thinking before
that there might be
nothing more.

CAN'T GET ENOUGH

It's got to be something
you can't get enough of;

if there's an end to it,
you'll be frustrated.

If there's not an end to it,
you'll still be frustrated,
but at least you'll carry on.

ASCETIC GLUTTON

Mindful on a morsel
when you're starving.

But what about, on a mouthful
when your stomach is full?

Can the fortunate glutton
be mindful, as an ascetic monk?

THINGS FALL APART

Things hold together
only if you glance quickly,
and then avert your eyes.

Otherwise you see, that
nothing stays the same;

everything is entangled,
melting and blurring
into everything else;

hard to tell where
one thing stops
and the next begins,

like a child's watercolor
that melts at the edges
of each brushstroke.

SLIPPED INTO CHAINS

I just hope
it was our freedom
which we were after
all this time.

Otherwise it seems
we may have slipped
into an accidental bondage
whilst chasing after
a breakage thereof.

LOCKED OUT

You get locked out,
like going to prison
or being stranded.

And you try to
recreate everything
in terms of what
you knew before.

But it's not the same
and you're not sure
if you even want to
go on living anymore.

When there's a world
you don't get to
be a part of;

you want your
old world back
or no world at all.

CAUSAL PRISON

We are born into bondage,
only able to experience
the few causal reactions

that are determined
by the space and time
which we're rationed.

So that our freedom
in the expanse of
such a vast universe

turned out to be
only so free

as salt in the sea
or a train on tracks,

as leaves on a tree
or a bee stuck in wax.

BODY ANCHOR

I can certainly be
myself, physically;

when I close my eyes
and plug my ears,
I still feel my hands.

When I open my eyes,
I am what I see.

When I unplug my ears,
I am what I hear.

In my memory
and imagination,
I can extend elsewhere;

but my body stays put,
like an anchor.

FORGE YOUR CHAINS

Forge your own chains.
Bind yourself to something.
Work in the fields and reap what you sew.

In order to work toward a point in space,
you must be confined and bordered;
let these constructions be your own.

Point yourself.
Build the banks of your own river.
You will flow no matter what;

whether it is all over and indiscriminate,
or driven with the force of a flood
—that is up to you.

MOMENTUM

Once you've put it into motion, then you just have to keep up and let it carry you along.

The difficulty comes when you want to change directions, after you've built up some speed,

so that you have to break the whole system, just to slow it down enough to change course.

Then you get out ahead to lay new track and spend some time rebuilding the machine,

and you sit there and huff and puff to catch your breath and gather some steam,

until you've set it into motion once more, then lay back and relax, as it begins again to carry you along.

GENERALLY SPECIFIC

Only so much can be said specifically,
while much more can be said generally,
because generalities can become much
—different, to each of many who hear.
Anything specific, is the same to all.

ABSOLUTES

There must be absolutes.
Because to say there are none,
is itself an absolute.

Or, maybe, it is to speak,
that is the only untruth.
To say nothing at all, is truth.

BETTER LEFT JUST TO BE

There are some mysteries better left that way. Nothings that we're better off not whispering, no matter how sweet. Whimpers that won't whine quite contrary to canon as we want them to. When it's all up to the moment just to be, ignoring our nagging to describe and box and tie it up package and parcel, when it's really so much wider than that. Better left unsaid, these things. Better left just to be.

IF WE KNEW

Then it would be
like looking at a map
and seeing the path
drawn out, so clearly
that you've almost
traveled it already
and see little point
in leaving home.

PROPHECY

Like a cup that fills itself,
it wouldn't have been
such a thing, as you believed,
if you hadn't believed in it
in such a way, that made it so.

AN OBJECTIVE TO START WITH

You can chop up a tree and make it into a house, but there first has to be a tree. Or, you can roast a marshmallow and put it on a graham with chocolate, but there first has to be a marshmallow.

Similarly, you can write Lewis-Carroll-nonsense and made-up words, but there first has to be the English language. Or, you can be an anarchist and a vagabond, but there first has to be a society mainly comprised of those who follow the rules.

You can have a wolf in sheep's clothing, but there first have to be sheep. You can truly revolt, only after you've played along.

You can have art, but there first has to be reality. You can have the opposite end of any dualist notion, but there first has to be the other.

On one hand, you can subjectively play with anything to make it your own. On the other, you need something, an objective, to start with.

ISNESS

To spread if it does;
needing what I have;
knowing what can be;
what happens will surely
—what is, is what is.

~9~
MICRODOSING

FIRE

When you need a boost
just to get over the edge
like a match to start a fire,

though the small stick
will be used and spent
and even broken,

a sacrifice is made
for the flame of a log fire

that spreads and spreads
even into a whole forest,

like leaving the house
with a candle still burning
and it catches the drapes,

the bookshelf and everything
you have is consumed,

because you forgot
to snuff out the fire
that you started yourself.

HOT AIR BALLOON

When you forget about everything
and blow so much hot air
into your own balloon,

until there's no breath
left in your lungs
and you start to fall—

and at first, you know
it is only temporary,

but at some point
so far beneath,

you start to wonder
if you'll ever rise again.

So much time in the dark,
and deeper, darker, all the while,

you start to wonder
if you'll ever be the same.

BOMB OFF

Go ahead and bomb off, everything is safe here, you needn't worry, go ahead.

Go ahead and bomb off, what you need you have—there is food in the fridge, your bed is here, the door is locked, and nobody's around.

Go ahead and bomb off, don't think about anything outside of this room, and if your mind starts to wander, then just remember to breathe.

Go ahead and bomb off, cover up the clocks and don't think about the time, put your wristwatch on the shelf and close the blinds.

Go ahead and bomb off, today is your day, bomb off, it's alright, when you come back you'll still be yourself, don't worry.

Go ahead and bomb off, keep your hands and feet inside the cabin, and if you start to think, just breathe, you'll be alright.

Go ahead and bomb off, read this if you get worried, everything is okay, you'll be alright, you great big baby, you'll be fine.

Go ahead and bomb off, you'll be alright, you great big baby, you'll be fine.

4:37AM SPEECH-TO-TEXT ABOUT SOBRIETY

In such sobriety everything is clear as it should be similar evening to the drug that distorts reality such that with the drug around you need edges but I've seen show shark sobriety sharpens the edges 13 so round allowing me to see wrinkles the hardwood floor in the end it screws noticing things I wouldn't have before stopping on my walk home to start something I walked by $100 but not noticed is beautiful being myself as a human should be but losing touch with something more that being human prevents us from accessingAt least not consistently only allowing to see as recluses like a drug guy but in the case you're going to give that up so Briody allows your godly version of being human.

SOBER GLUE

I travel to this other world. So that the true test of my life is making the journey back. The other world is entropy and chaos, creativity and love—but poison, without an occasional dose of glue, from the reality where I must occasionally return.

The real reality that I have learned to stop calling "real," or at least not any more "real" than the other. This reality (as we will call it for now) of names and concepts, is what sustains my physical body. The principal commodity here is a very certain kind of glue that keeps all my molecules together and maintains the cohesion of my sense of self.

I huff on this glue, walking in straight lines on the sidewalk, learning and obeying the laws of nature, being careful and avoiding danger, eating and sleeping. I huff and huff until I'm strong enough to take another hit and travel. At which point the earth tips upside down and I fall off the sidewalk into outer space.

Out here, in my beloved other world (which I should stop calling "other," if I have stopped calling reality "real") a new creative force pulls me in all directions. It is only the glue that keeps me together.

I revel in being stretched, but only so far, before my molecules are spread wide enough to make permanently impossible a return journey to the reality of sidewalks and safety—which is when, with all my strength, I pull myself together and return.

SO MUCH

so much so much so much so much so much so much
so much so much so much so much so much so much
so much so much so much so much so much so much
so much so much so much so much so much so much
so much so much so much so much so much so much
so much so much so much so much so much so much
so much so much so much so much so much so much
so much so much so much so much so much so much
so much so much so much so much so much so much
so much so much so much so much so much so much
so much so much so much so much so much so much
so much so much so much so much so much so much
so much so much so much so much so much so much
so much so much so much so much so much so much
so much so much so much so much so much so much
so much so much so much so much so much so much
so much so much so much so much so much so much
so much so much so much so much so much so much
so much so much so much so much so much so much
so much so much so much so much so much so much
so much so much so much so much so much so much
so much so much so much so much so much so much
so much so much so much so much so much so much
so much so much so much so much so much so much
so much so much so much so much so much so much
so much so much so much so much so much so much
so much so much so much so much so much so much
so much so much so much so much so much so much
so much so much so much so much so much so much
so much so much so much so much so much so much
so much so much so much so much so much so much
so much so much so much so much so much so much

ALL AT ONCE

all at once all at once all at once all at once all at once
all at once all at once all at once all at once all at once
all at once all at once all at once all at once all at once
all at once all at once all at once all at once all at once
all at once all at once all at once all at once all at once
all at once all at once all at once all at once all at once
all at once all at once all at once all at once all at once
all at once all at once all at once all at once all at once
all at once all at once all at once all at once all at once
all at once all at once all at once all at once all at once
all at once all at once all at once all at once all at once
all at once all at once all at once all at once all at once
all at once all at once all at once all at once all at once
all at once all at once all at once all at once all at once
all at once all at once all at once all at once all at once
all at once all at once all at once all at once all at once
all at once all at once all at once all at once all at once
all at once all at once all at once all at once all at once
all at once all at once all at once all at once all at once
all at once all at once all at once all at once all at once
all at once all at once all at once all at once all at once
all at once all at once all at once all at once all at once
all at once all at once all at once all at once all at once
all at once all at once all at once all at once all at once
all at once all at once all at once all at once all at once
all at once all at once all at once all at once all at once
all at once all at once all at once all at once all at once
all at once all at once all at once all at once all at once
all at once all at once all at once all at once all at once
all at once all at once all at once all at once all at once
all at once all at once all at once all at once all at once
all at once all at once all at once all at once all at once

MACRODOSE

I dose myself up too high
and stretch out my shirt
to make a parachute
for the way back down.

~10~
EGOMANIA

MARGINS

When it really doesn't
want to be that way;

so much, I push off
and forget to relent

even when my sanity
is shouting, *no!*

At the margins of what
keeps me together,

even though I want to
fall apart all the time;

I hold together until
right when oblivion

promises more than
remaining myself.

GOING IN A CIRCLE

It is in the passing from
one moment to the next,

each of which I fill with
the results of my desires.

The desires themselves
I can never remember;

only the results of them
play out where I can see.

So when I end up in a mess
and feel the desire to change,

I can't remember if it was
the very same desire for change
that got me here in the first place.

FORGOTTEN

Go ahead and think about it
just long enough to forget.

And if you forget, oh well,
you will have forgotten;

you will remember someday,
or you won't, but no matter,
you will have forgotten.

SMALL, STUPID LIE

I lied today. It was a small, stupid lie. I lied about something that happened in college. In truth, it was a story that my friend told me. I lied and said it was me that was there. I feel bad about it now. I wish I could take it back. I said it just to impress the person who I was talking to. But it wasn't worth it.

GIVE AND TAKE

I think I have given
only to realize that,
like every other, equal
and opposite reaction,
I have first taken.

LIKE A LEAF

I get caught up
like a leaf in the wind
and let it carry me along.

UNORIGINAL

In trying to live a life
not yet lived before

I've ended up living
a life lived many times

by those before me
who tried to live a life
not yet lived before.

NEW NEEDS

I spend my time working
just to rest again.

I wait in between meals
to get hungry.

I let myself hurt
to feel pleasure soon after.

I satisfy my needs
until I'm all out of needs
and then I wait for new needs.

EMPTY BRAIN

It's a bunch of thoughts fighting for my attention. Like a classroom, when all the students raise their hands at once, and the teacher doesn't know who to call on. They all collide heads and explode and nobody wins. So I end up thinking of nothing all the time, until you ask me and I don't know what to say.

FULLY EMPTY

I feel full
in the sense
that I am empty.

I've let it all go
and it's out there,

more than I could've
held within myself.

And now there's space
to let more in.

MORE WILL COME

Let it all grow and change
outside of yourself.

Hold only what is given to you,
only long enough to give it away.

You are a sieve, that must occasionally
be turned upside down and emptied,

even of what you've caught.
Let everything else flow through,

and do not long for it to come again.
More will come.

~11~
THREE FOR SOCIETY

GODFUL

For the first time in a million years
beating blood meets far away light,

through eyes that shimmer
like stained-glass windows

in a high-ceilinged church
built from a jungle of primal life.

At first my beating heart complains
and wants to go back to the wild.

Once I manage to wrestle it down,
I read a missal and hymn-listen;

it beats slower and learns of
more than one God to beat for.

A PEASANT'S WEALTH

They say the good steak is what melts like butter in your mouth, but I like the tough stuff that you can chew like bubble gum; they say it's for peasants, but *bah*, what good is a steak that melts and is gone?

They say the good cheese stinks and the good wine tastes like metal, but *bah*, I want a cheese I can eat and a wine I can drink.

They say the good life is sitting around doing nothing all day, but *bah*, I'd be bored in the first minute. Give me the yoke; let me work up an appetite.

They say the rich sit way up high, but *bah*, put me in the dirt where I came from.

EDGES THAT CUT

All around us sharp edges were breaking down our motivations to be anything that might bleed past the cuts. Most of us didn't have the guts to try, but we might have known if we did that the edges were soft as skin, not like normal kitchen knives that would cut you for sure, but instead more like the thorns on a pineapple or the needles on a porcupine—full of dynamic life and happy to have a conversation with you about their place in the world if you'd only ask.

But we never did ask most of the time, owing to our memories of a cut in the kitchen, shuddering not only to remember the pain from the cut, but more so the drop of blood in the stew that the whole family was counting on, so that our pain is twofold—and only the first is selfish, whereas the second has to do with our place among the others. Even if we were to brave the physical pain, we still wouldn't want to risk our place.

SAFE HERE

With your ears shut out
from what everyone hears;

here, where we're together;
or there, where it's all one,

all you—lonely, if not for
what you create for yourself.

Come back to us dear,
and hear the headless harken;

the waves that don't break
save the lack for a beach;

the slack for a rope
that hangs itself;

the selfsame love
that hands its own shoulders;

and all for what you wanted,
but never found out there.

Come back to us dear,
you'll be safe here.

LONELY AT THE TOP

Most of the time,
we do the same thing

as everyone else,
completely unoriginal;

sometimes we break through
and really get into it

and hoot and holler
thinking that we've done it

—gotten ahead of the pack
and can now revel

in the brave sense
of pushing the frontier

all on our own,
until we look around

and realize that
we're all on our own.

EMPATHY

As I walk around the city
and people pass by,

I try to catch their eyes
and live their lives

just for the moment
that I look at them.

I almost bang my knee
on a fire hydrant,

watching where
they're going,

forgetting
to be myself.

I see that
there's a little

of everyone,
in anyone.

EMPATHY #2

Seeing from a door knob's perspective,
from the sun's eyes looking down.
Feeling what it's like to be a sound wave.

Loving with the dying heart of a soldier.
Thinking with the desperate mind of an outlaw.

Running like rain water doomed for the gutter.
Sleeping like sacks of potatoes in a farm truck.
Kissing with lover mouths outside the café.
Hanging like a handle waiting to be useful.

Competing like cars on the freeway.
Remembering like an epic told over and over.
Hurting like alcohol in an open wound.
Holding on like a palm tree in a hurricane.

Feeling with fir tree fingertips.
Learning like a library bookshelf.
Waiting like a dog for his owner.
Focusing like a lion on a hunt.

Loose and flow like a river
and crumple like a chip bag,
then build like Rome
and stand like a mountain.

~12~
STREAM OF NONSENSE

IT COULD BE NOTHING

I came about it backwards;
rather than one being one
and the next to be next,

I picked up arbitrarily
a piece of the whole

and asked, what could
this otherwise be?

MOON MINDS

Spending time
with a wasting whine
that waxes off, not on;

until there clears
some subtle fear
that what was
wasn't there.

Only then,
where compass spins
and map men
know no longer,

does truth reveal
what hearts can't feel
and only moon
minds ponder.

LILY PAD REVOLUTION

When you don't really know
what you want to say
about dragging out
a paramount,

keep it consistent
and nag a lake
for the fish on bottom
to bubble up a complaint

that makes enough sense
to rally the lily pads
against the dam.

RAIN CLOUDS

Up along
the water skies
I left a little letter.

It said that so
was what you know
and nothing would get better.

So I was scared
without you here
and started to expect,

that what was next
would carry less
and rain down clouds elect.

GLASS CASTLE

A delicate system
of glass trusses
sure shimmers

but holds for
not much more
than the light.

Even if you build
softly and slowly,

the higher you go
there is a risk run

of breaking before
you reach the sun.

BOW AND ARROW

When homeward arrows
beckon stronger bows
for a target that exceeds
in space, the hunger
of the archer's quiver.

DOUBLE YOUS

Woken on walked up
whimple washed waves
—these double yous
keep coming back to me.

MARBLE JARS

Epic animal sights
after four beer flights

seeing eyes their whites
crying flies and mites

only simple slow
powder soft as snow

it would seem there are
fewer marble jars.

TRUTH IS OVERRATED

Don't think like that:
like you can't go on,
or it won't be much longer,

or it's not true,
or the end is near,
or nothing matters,

or anything else
that might be true,
but doesn't help you
by its truth.

MIDNIGHT FLOWERS

Just when I think
the poetry has dried up,

and all I've left
in my forlorn life
is a tragic trudging forward;

just then, I'm up in the night,
with flowers bursting from my chest.

No soil beneath my rib cage
and no sunlight in my room;

but nevertheless,
here are these flowers,

brightening my midnight life
and making smile

a face that hasn't
for quite a while.

"Make your interests gradually wider and more impersonal, until bit by bit the walls of the ego recede, and your life becomes increasingly merged in the universal life. An individual human existence should be like a river—small at first, narrowly contained within its banks, and rushing passionately past rocks and over waterfalls. Gradually the river grows wider, the banks recede, the waters flow more quietly, and in the end, without any visible break, they become merged in the sea, and painlessly lose their individual being."

— Bertrand Russell, "How to Grow Old"

Made in the USA
San Bernardino, CA
17 June 2019